Good Morning, Takaya

Good Morning, Takaya

CHERYL ALEXANDER and ALEX VAN TOL

RMB

Good morning, Takaya,
lone wolf on the bluff.

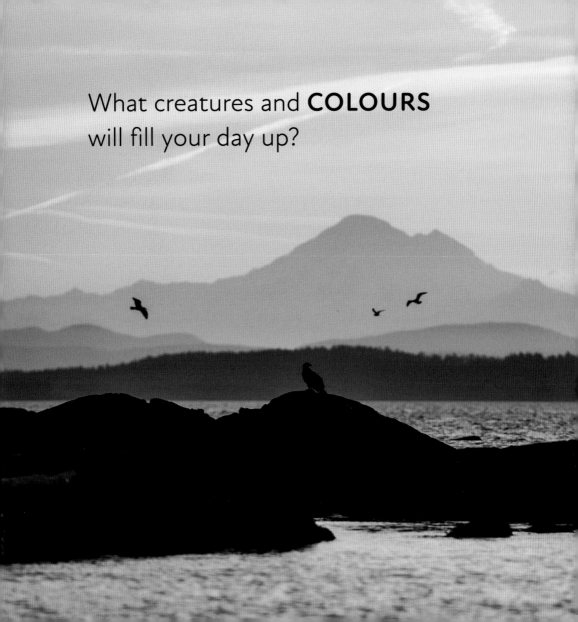

What creatures and **COLOURS**
will fill your day up?

The heron stands tall in the **ORANGE** sunrise.
Like you, this hunter is patient and wise.

You pause to watch geese
in the **PURPLE** wildflowers.
You'd follow that wee
YELLOW gosling for hours!

A bald eagle soars
through a vibrant **BLUE** sky.
The moon is still out —
are you wondering why?

Your two watchful eyes
spot a wee murrelet.
Her **BLACK** and **WHITE** feathers
are fluffy and wet.

I see you, Takaya,
keeping watch out of sight.
Your fur shines like GOLD
in the warm morning light.

High up in a tree
sits a silent barred owl.
Will her **BROWN** feathers fly
if you let out a howl?

A plump **ROSY** apple
holds fast to the tree.
The spider's at home,
but too tiny to see!

Through bright **PURPLE** camas blooms dotting the grass, you look like you've found something tasty at last!

It's only a gull
and her fluffy **GREY** baby.
Keep hunting, Takaya.
You'll find something, maybe.

Perhaps you would share
in this otter's noon meal.
I know you like fish —
but your favourite is seal.

You wander the island,
marking on logs.
Who's watching you now?
It's a little **GREEN** frog!

The swift-moving hummingbird builds her soft nest. **WHITE** fluff from the bulrushes seems to work best.

Your howl fills the forest
with notes long and low.
Are you asking a question,
or saying hello?

With **BLACK** glossy wings,
Raven shows up to play.
All sorts of wild friends
come to share in your day.

You've wandered your island
and now you must rest.
Perhaps near the YELLOW
wildflowers is best.

You wake from your doze
to see WHITE seagulls splashing.
Held tight in their beaks,
SILVER herring are flashing.

In the kelp beds nearby, a sleek seal mum of GREY
Sings a song to her pup at the end of the day.

Contented companions, two orcas glide by.
The water shines COPPER as evening draws nigh.

Hunt stealthily now,
in the **ORANGE** evening rays.
A gift from the Earth,
you will have food for days.

PINK light warms the shores
of your islands, my friend.
It's a wonderful way
for your full day to end.

It's time now, Takaya,
for curling up tight.
I loved sharing your day,
and now wish you good night.